I AM NOT A LABEL

WIDE EYED EDITIONS

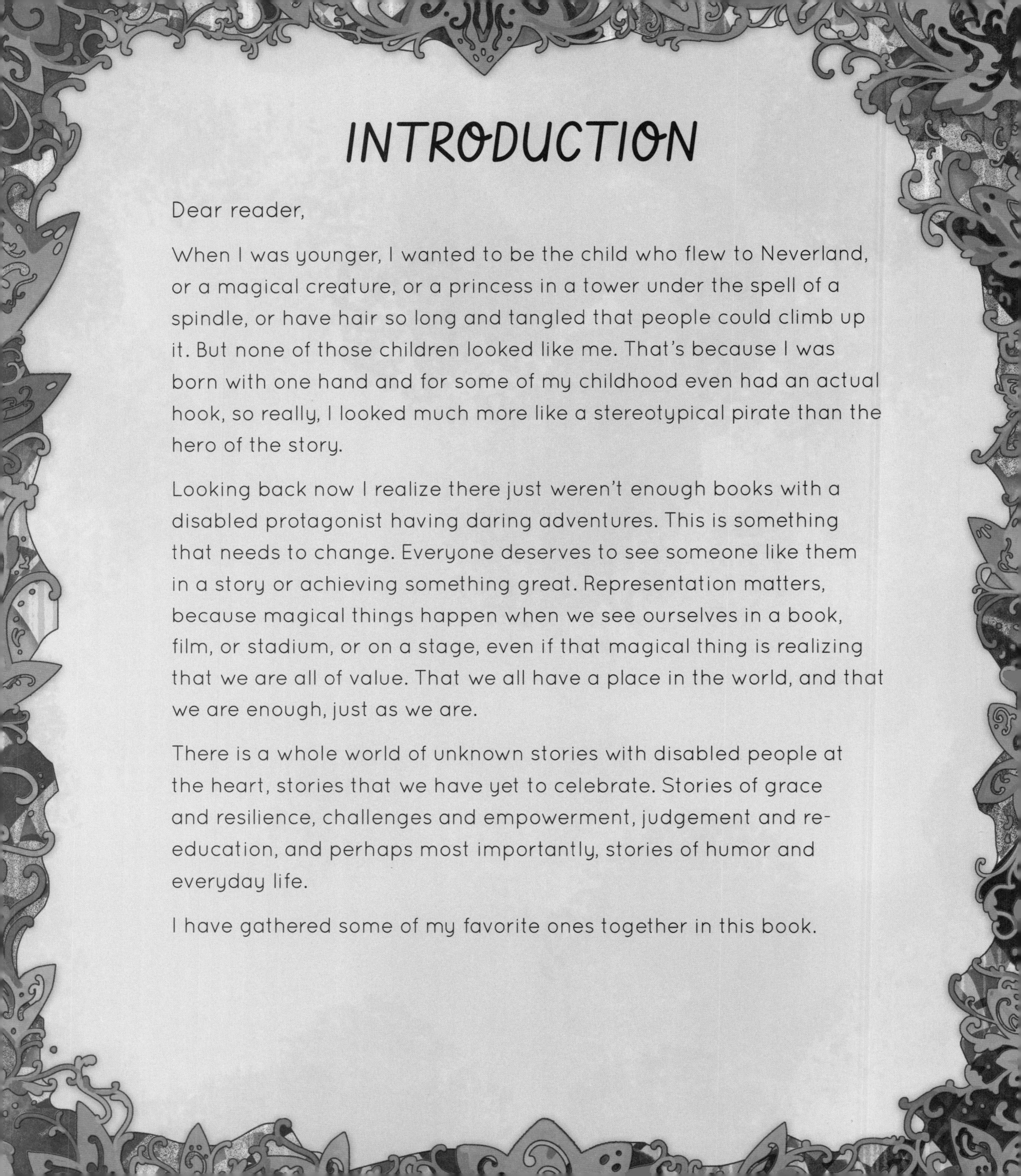

INTRODUCTION

Dear reader,

When I was younger, I wanted to be the child who flew to Neverland, or a magical creature, or a princess in a tower under the spell of a spindle, or have hair so long and tangled that people could climb up it. But none of those children looked like me. That's because I was born with one hand and for some of my childhood even had an actual hook, so really, I looked much more like a stereotypical pirate than the hero of the story.

Looking back now I realize there just weren't enough books with a disabled protagonist having daring adventures. This is something that needs to change. Everyone deserves to see someone like them in a story or achieving something great. Representation matters, because magical things happen when we see ourselves in a book, film, or stadium, or on a stage, even if that magical thing is realizing that we are all of value. That we all have a place in the world, and that we are enough, just as we are.

There is a whole world of unknown stories with disabled people at the heart, stories that we have yet to celebrate. Stories of grace and resilience, challenges and empowerment, judgement and re-education, and perhaps most importantly, stories of humor and everyday life.

I have gathered some of my favorite ones together in this book.

This is an anthology of tales about disabled artists, athletes, activists, thinkers, writers, performers, and dreamers, finding joy, normality, and wonder in a world that deems us "different" (as though this something bad). In this book I have choose to use what is called identity-first language, which means I say "disabled person" instead of "a person with a disability". Neither is wrong, or offensive, but it is important to remember that people are disabled by society and do not need to be fixed. If there are any words in the book that you're not sure about, there is a glossary at the end to help.

Each person in this book has led or continues to lead a fascinating life, often overcoming misconceptions and prejudice to do so. I hope you will love reading their stories. I hope they will show you that we are all more than just a label, and that whoever you are, disabled or not, there are no limits to your dreams.

We all have the power to shine our own light. Everyone deserves to live in an inclusive and accessible world and feel like they belong. A world that embraces difference rather than tries to hide it, and a world where every person's story is valid.

Big love,

Cerrie Burnell

xxx

BEETHOVEN

1770-1827 — Composer

A long time ago in the modest town of Bonn in Germany, there lived a boy named Ludwig van Beethoven. He was born to a humble family, and music and melodies filled his heart. But as Ludwig grew up, there was a lot of sickness in his family.

Ludwig's father had wanted to become a musician himself but never managed to. He saw his son had extraordinary musical talent and made Ludwig practise the piano for hours each day. Ludwig's mother and father both died young, and he was left to look after his younger brothers.

As the head of the family, Ludwig began playing the viola in an orchestra to earn money. He understood music naturally and began composing moving and daring music for the orchestra. As well as composing, he taught music to gifted children.

As his name became known, Ludwig moved to the vibrant city of Vienna, where his fame grew. He composed exquisite scores for ballet, opera, and huge, sweeping orchestral symphonies.

He had a wild, unstoppable heart and fell in love many times. But each time, his loves were from very wealthy families. Their parents did not want their children marrying someone as poor as Ludwig.

At 25 Ludwig began to struggle to hear, and after a time he became profoundly deaf. When one of the best piano makers in England sent him a fabulous piano, he could not hear a single note.

Though sometimes this made Ludwig melancholy it did not interrupt his composing. Music was in his soul and it spilled out of him, like stories made from sound. Although he couldn't hear his creations, he knew the notes by heart, and poured all the sadness, regret, courage, and joy he had into his scores. When his compositions were performed, Ludwig could feel the vibrations of the music through his whole body.

He wrote a letter to his brothers, explaining his determination not to let his disability stop him. Some of his most famous works were written at a furious pace during the last ten years of his life, when he could not hear at all.

He died at the age of 56 and is regarded as one of the most innovative and important composers of all time. His music lives on and is performed by orchestras all over the world.

GUSTAV KIRCHHOFF

1824-1887 — Physicist

A long time ago in a place called Prussia, which is now part of modern-day Russia, there lived a man named Gustav. His family belonged to an exceptional community of intellectuals and great thinkers, who would stay up late into the night debating the issues that faced the world at that moment.

Gustav found it difficult to walk and used crutches to help him, or sometimes he preferred to use a wheelchair. The thing that people noticed most about him was his extraordinary and unusually brilliant scientific mind.

Gustav had a knack for understanding complicated scientific theories. At school he loved physics and math. He was always reading and learning, and so he found it easy to do well on exams. His family knew he was a hard worker and was destined for great things. But not everything was simple for Gustav—he lived during a time when most places weren't set up for wheelchair users, so it was hard for him to move around.

When he went to university, he made friends with one of his tutors, a man named Franz Neumann. While he studied with Neumann, Gustav began to make miraculous discoveries. He developed circuits, found ways to analyze the Sun and the speed at which light travels, and created what he called "the three laws of spectroscopy."

With all this success to his name, Gustav moved to Berlin to further his research. There he fell deeply in love with a woman named Clara, and soon married her.

They had five children and were terribly happy, but sadly Clara died young. After that, Gustav raised his children alone, having to balance this alongside his research. It was difficult, but he managed. After a time, he remarried, and with the extra support of his wife, he was able to work more than before. He traveled and gave lectures and continued to achieve astonishing success, changing quantum physics forever.

His life was lit by the brightness of his discoveries and the study of light. He became famous for his magnificent intellect and extraordinary mind.

HENRI MATISSE

1869-1954 — Artist

Once, long ago in northern France, a grain merchant and his wealthy wife had a baby named Henri. Henri was a bright and studious young man and when he finished school he set off to Paris to study law. But Henri contracted appendicitis and had to come home to recover. To distract him, his mother gave him a set of paints, which would change the course of his life.

As he painted from bed, Henri discovered a kind of paradise and fell completely in love with art. He decided to become an artist, but this wildly disappointed his father.

Henri rushed back to Paris to learn his new craft. He wanted to perfect every technique—printmaking, sculpture and collage—but his true love was painting. At first the colors Henri used were muted and calm, but after he befriended an artist named John Russell he was inspired to use riotous, outrageous colors.

He painted everyday things he came across, such as vases of sunflowers, women with hats, or the view from his open window. Henri and some friends showed their work in a gallery. They used colors in such an exciting and strange way that people called them the "wild beasts."

Henri's friend, the art collector Gertrude Stein, who was a powerhouse of the art world, introduced Henri to an artist named Pablo Picasso. The two became friendly rivals, always challenging each other to be more daring.

Henri lived a life filled with art and parties and fabulous fun. He had a daughter with Caroline, who was a model, and later he married Amelie, with whom he had two sons. They moved to the French Riviera, where they kept doves and had three cats who ate brioche for breakfast.

After a time, Henri became very ill with cancer, and after surgery, he spent most of his time in bed or a wheelchair. This made painting a challenge, so he changed his technique so he could work from bed. He painted big squares of color and then cut shapes out of them. He arranged them to make superb collages, calling it "painting with scissors." He often included cut-outs of his beloved doves in these artworks. His new way of making pictures was revolutionary and all came out of his need to adapt his working practice.

In this time of healing, Henri created some of his best-loved work. He lived a long and fulfilled life, just as colorful as his artistic creations.

ELIZA SUGGS

1876-1908 — Author

Long ago in the hot Southern United States lived a happy family with four children. Their parents had lived through the time of slavery, and were determined to raise them to be loving and resilient. The youngest was Eliza.

One day, when Eliza was very young, she began crying out in pain. It took her mother all day to discover what was wrong: Eliza had broken a bone. Her family took her straight to the doctor, who helped her to heal, but it wasn't long before more of her bones began to splinter.

Eliza's body was as fragile as china—even walking could cause her to break a bone. Without a wheelchair the only way she could get around was to be pushed in a stroller. As she grew older she could not play in the sun—instead she liked to sit by her window and watch the world outside.

No one knew what was causing Eliza's condition, but it was eventually diagnosed as osteomalacia, a disease that weakened her bones and muscles. When she was six, her parents had funeral clothes made for her as they feared she would die very soon.

But Eliza wanted to live and be in control of her life! She wanted to feel the kiss of the sun on her face, the wind in her hair and the splash of rain on her skin. And more than anything she wanted to learn about the world beyond her window.

When her family moved, a teacher gave Eliza a place in her class. But the classroom was up a flight of stairs and impossible for her to reach. Then a family friend gave Eliza a wheelchair, which gave her more freedom and confidence. Each morning her sister pushed her to school. Then, the other children helped her up the stairs, so she could learn and laugh with her friends.

Eliza became highly educated, something that was rare for black women in this time. Her father was a devoted preacher and Eliza and her sister Kate soon began accompanying him, so Eliza could speak about her difficulties and triumphs and how her faith had kept her heart hopeful.

People loved to hear Eliza speak. She was inspired to write down her experiences and published a book telling the story of her life called *Shadows and Sunshine*.

Eliza died at the age of 32, having lived a life rich with travel and literature and having experienced the power that came from telling her truth.

HELEN KELLER

1880-1968 — Author and Educator

Helen grew up in the Deep South and when she was very young, she contracted an illness which meant she became deaf and blind. Her family did everything they could to support her, and although Helen sometimes felt as if she was "at sea in a dense fog," she used her quick hands to make up signs to communicate. The cook in her family home had a daughter who was Helen's friend and understood her hand signs. By the time Helen was seven, she had invented 60 signs.

Sometimes Helen was very frustrated because it was so hard to communicate, and she found her frustration hard to control. She would throw tantrums, kicking anyone who came near. As Helen grew older, her parents looked for a way to educate their daughter, and travelled to Boston to the Perkins School for the Blind. They recommended a tutor named Anne Sullivan who agreed to be Helen's governess.

Anne came to Helen's house on the 5th of March 1887, a day Helen described as "my soul's birthday." Helen had not realized that every object in the world had a word. It was only when Anne taught her to spell out "water" with her fingers, while running water gently over her hands, that she understood. Helen at once demanded to know the signs for everything!

Determined to communicate with the world, Helen began learning to speak in a clear, eloquent voice. As she couldn't hear the sounds she needed to make, this took her many years to accomplish.

With Anne Sullivan at her side, Helen was able to attend school and then college, meeting many people who inspired Helen on her journey. At the age of 21, she wrote *The Story of My Life* and travelled all over the world, speaking about her achievements and winning people's hearts.

Helen fought to raise the profile of disabled people and became an advocate for women's rights. She set up the Helen Keller Institute and co-founded the American Civil Liberties Union.

She won many awards and accolades and gave speeches around the world. Her book was turned into a TV series and Broadway play and she became a world-renowned activist, championing tenacity and imagination.

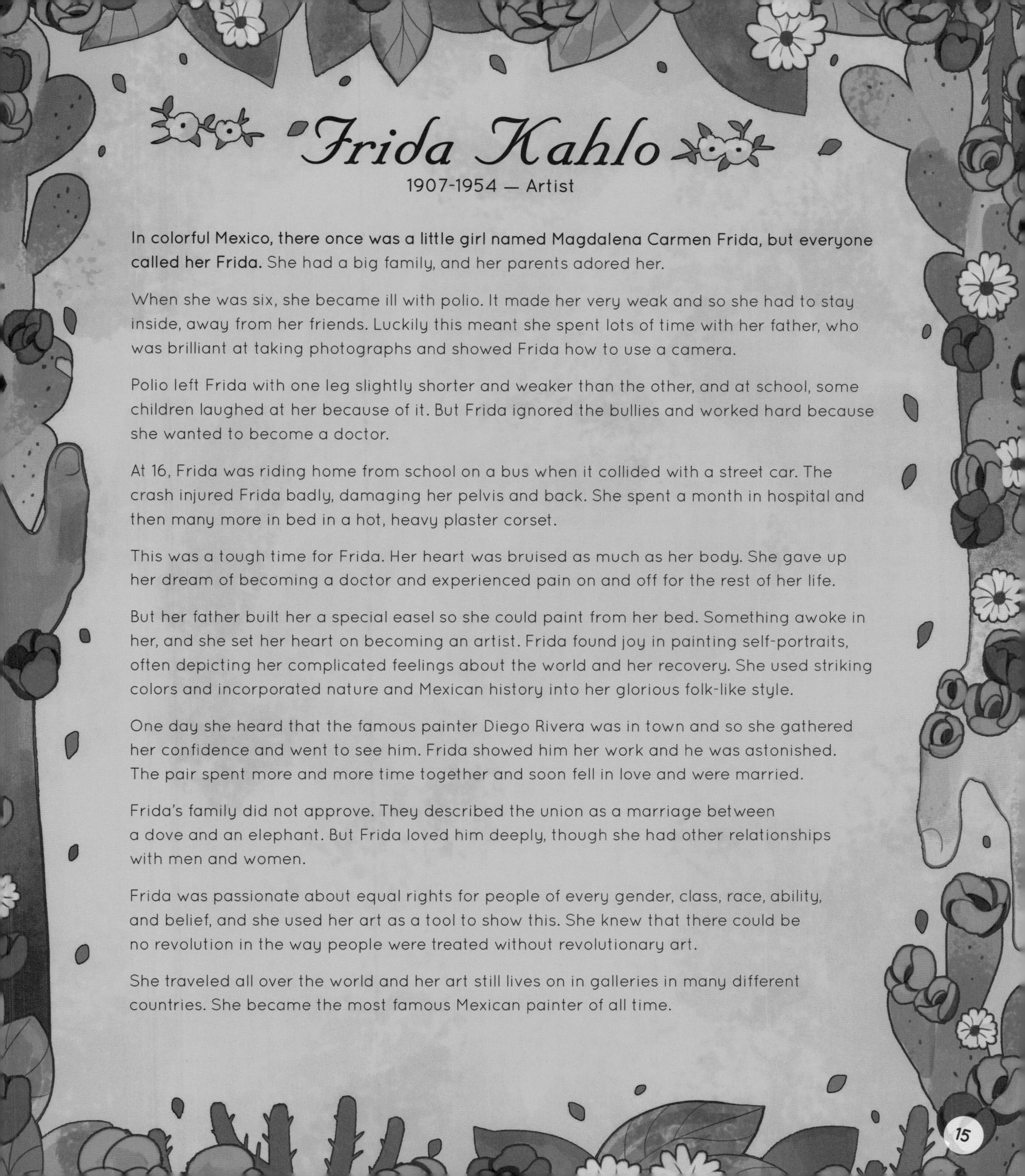

Frida Kahlo

1907-1954 — Artist

In colorful Mexico, there once was a little girl named Magdalena Carmen Frida, but everyone called her Frida. She had a big family, and her parents adored her.

When she was six, she became ill with polio. It made her very weak and so she had to stay inside, away from her friends. Luckily this meant she spent lots of time with her father, who was brilliant at taking photographs and showed Frida how to use a camera.

Polio left Frida with one leg slightly shorter and weaker than the other, and at school, some children laughed at her because of it. But Frida ignored the bullies and worked hard because she wanted to become a doctor.

At 16, Frida was riding home from school on a bus when it collided with a street car. The crash injured Frida badly, damaging her pelvis and back. She spent a month in hospital and then many more in bed in a hot, heavy plaster corset.

This was a tough time for Frida. Her heart was bruised as much as her body. She gave up her dream of becoming a doctor and experienced pain on and off for the rest of her life.

But her father built her a special easel so she could paint from her bed. Something awoke in her, and she set her heart on becoming an artist. Frida found joy in painting self-portraits, often depicting her complicated feelings about the world and her recovery. She used striking colors and incorporated nature and Mexican history into her glorious folk-like style.

One day she heard that the famous painter Diego Rivera was in town and so she gathered her confidence and went to see him. Frida showed him her work and he was astonished. The pair spent more and more time together and soon fell in love and were married.

Frida's family did not approve. They described the union as a marriage between a dove and an elephant. But Frida loved him deeply, though she had other relationships with men and women.

Frida was passionate about equal rights for people of every gender, class, race, ability, and belief, and she used her art as a tool to show this. She knew that there could be no revolution in the way people were treated without revolutionary art.

She traveled all over the world and her art still lives on in galleries in many different countries. She became the most famous Mexican painter of all time.

JOHN NASH

1928-2015 — Mathematician

Not so long ago in the state of Virginia lived a young boy called John. John was a math genius with a brilliant and complex mind.

As John grew into a young man he excelled in all his studies, winning scholarships and gaining a place at Princeton University. Here he became known as "The Phantom of Fine Hall" as he would be up all night, wandering the shadowy corridors, wildly scrawling equations on every blackboard, determined to work them out.

This dedication helped John to become an extraordinary scholar, but it also meant that his sleep was disturbed, and his understanding of reality became blurred. John often felt very alone or sad, or believed that other people were plotting against him, when in fact they weren't.

As John's life and wondrous career progressed, the state of his mental health declined and became overwhelming. He had a son with a nurse, and then eventually married a woman he had fallen deeply in love with named Alicia.

John and Alicia were very happy together. During Alicia's pregnancy John began to feel very distanced from the world and was admitted to a hospital.

John spent much of his life in and out of the hospital receiving treatment for psychosis. He did not like these stays and was always keen to get home to his wife where he could live a quiet, peaceful existence. Nor did he like any of the medication he was given to manage his mental health. He felt it dulled the sharpness of his mind. Though John found his mental health condition exhausting, he also knew that his magnificent mind was a great gift, which he cherished.

With the support of his loving wife, John lived an extraordinary life. He made peace with his challenging mental health condition and discovered theorems that no one had imagined before. His work used math to explain real-life situations, such as how people compete against each other or work together, and showed ways to predict the chance of complex things happening. He became the subject of a book and film about his own life called *A Beautiful Mind*. He was the only person ever to win the Nobel Memorial Prize and the Abel Prize in the same year.

John's complexity of thought made difficult equations that no one had managed to tackle before seem easy.

q2
q3
B
x
y
p

STEPHEN HAWKING

1942-2018 — Theoretical Physicist

Stephen lived in Oxford, England, the City of Dreaming Spires, and he certainly had big dreams. He was brought up by his clever and slightly eccentric parents, surrounded by books.

Stephen was intelligent but he did not learn to read at his first school. The methods the school used didn't engage his incredible intelligence. But as soon as he changed schools, he learned very fast.

When his father was offered a new job, the family moved to St. Albans to a large, rundown house. While at school, with the help of his favorite teacher Mr. Tahta, Stephen and his friends built a computer from clock parts and an old telephone switchboard.

Stephen was a gifted mathematician and his nickname soon became "Einstein." He desperately wanted to study math at a university, but his parents wanted him to go to the prestigious Oxford University, where math wasn't offered. So instead Stephen chose to study physics and chemistry at Oxford.

Stephen found the work easy and a little dull and so he didn't study hard. Even so, he was still awarded first-class honors and went on to Cambridge to work on a PhD.

In Cambridge, he met a brilliant woman named Jane with whom he fell in love. Shortly after meeting her, when he was 21, Stephen was diagnosed with a type of motor neuron disease and given two years to live.

The diagnosis was initially devastating as the disease affected his muscles and meant that Stephen gradually lost the ability to speak, walk, and write. But it also made him focus on the things he wanted to do with his life. His love for Jane was another reason to live. He decided to complete as much groundbreaking work as he could, before his time ran out.

Stephen and Jane were married, and he became a father to three children. At the same time he gained a steady foothold in the difficult world of academia. He refused to speak publicly about his condition because he was determined to focus on his work. He used a computer to aid his speech and get his astonishing ideas across. He developed new theories about the nature of black holes, and the universe itself.

He often needed 24-hour care, but this did not stop him from becoming one of the most astonishing and respected academics of the century. Stephen lived until he was 76, outlasting the doctors' predictions by 53 years. He realized dreams and theories far beyond the dreaming spires of Oxford and is respected around the world.

TEMPLE GRANDIN

1947 — Professor of Animal Sciences

A little girl named Mary Temple Grandin was born in the state of Massachusetts. Temple did not learn to speak and when she was two, doctors wrongly diagnosed her with a brain injury. They recommended that she should live in a place far away from home where she would be given special care. But her mother was horrified by this. She didn't want her little girl to leave home! So, she asked some different doctors at Boston Children's Hospital who had very different advice.

They suggested that Temple have speech therapy. When Temple started nursery, all the teachers worked with the family to make the environment as welcoming as possible. Temple found it more calming if the room was light but not too brightly colored.

Temple's mother had strict rules and was determined that her daughter behave well and develop good social skills. Temple found it hard to make friends at school and was taunted by other children. One day she threw a book at another pupil and was asked to leave the school. Her mother moved her to a boarding school for children with additional needs. Temple found inspiration in the teachers she met there. One teacher named William Carlock helped her to invent a "hug box" to ease her anxieties. The hug box was a bit like a big armchair which gently compressed her, as if it were hugging her, and helped to make her feel calm. She also started making friends through shared interests in riding horses.

One summer, Temple stayed at her step-aunt's ranch, where she spent time with lots of animals and was amazed by how well she understood them. Temple empathised with the way the light and the dark, moving shadows startled the cows and how noise frightened them.

After this, Temple knew she could make animals' lives better. She went to university and became a leading specialist in animal behaviour. It was not until she was in her forties that she was diagnosed with autism. Since then, Temple has been one of the first women to speak openly and positively about living with autism. She hopes to show parents and teachers how to encourage incredible minds. If someone can't spell, it doesn't mean they won't one day build a rocket that will soar among the stars.

Temple continues to give insightful and necessary talks about how autistic people can live happily and authentically. Her skill for visual thinking helped her to understand animals. She is now a university professor.

STEVIE WONDER

1950 — Singer-songwriter

Stevland Hardaway Judkins was born in Michigan, USA, in the 1950s. Baby Stevie arrived six weeks early so the hospital kept him in an incubator to help him grow and develop. But the air in the incubator was so oxygen-rich that it affected his eyes, and he became completely blind.

Stevie grew up surrounded by his four brothers and one sister. They were noisy and creative. When he was four he moved to Detroit with his mother, brothers and sister. Stevie absolutely loved music! He came alive when he played the piano, harmonica, and drums and began singing in a local church choir. Stevie had a wonderful, soulful voice and a talent for writing his own songs. He marvelled at the world around him and wanted to share what he felt with others through his music. He said, "Just because a man lacks sight, doesn't mean he doesn't have vision."

As word of Stevie's gift traveled, he became recognized as a musical prodigy. He signed a record deal with Motown, the best record label at the time, when he was just 11. Stevie preferred performing in sunglasses as this meant the focus was on the music rather than his disability. He once said, "we all have ability, the difference is how you use it."

As a child Stevie's stage name was "Little Stevie Wonder," and two years into his career he topped the US Billboard Hot 100 with "Fingertips." It catapulted him to fame. As he grew up, Little Stevie became known simply as Stevie Wonder. He went on to break and make many more records and forge a monumental career.

Stevie has sold over 100 million records, won 25 Grammy Awards, and was the first African American and first Motown artist to win an Academy Award (an Oscar) for best original song.

In 1994, Stevie's very own star was unveiled on the Hollywood Walk of Fame. He is also included in the official Rock and Roll Hall of Fame, as well as the Song Writers' Hall of Fame. But Stevie is recognized for more than just his contribution to music. In 2009 he became a United Nations Messenger of Peace for his powerful and influential stance against racism. Stevie still performs all over the world in his signature, super-cool sunglasses.

Nabi Shaban

1953 — Actor and Writer

Some time ago in Jordan, a little baby boy was born to young parents who named him Nabil, which is Arabic for "Noble." (He was, after all, a descendant of Genghis Khan.) Nabil had osteogenesis imperfecta: his bones could break after only the gentlest knock. His mother noticed he looked slightly different than the other babies and thought it was because of something she had done.

The doctors weren't quite sure how they could help Nabil, so King Hussein of Jordan sent him to England to be treated at Queen Mary's Hospital for Children. He spent most of his childhood in a cot, but he dreamed about all the wild things he would do one day. Sometimes it was hard: his own teachers doubted what he could achieve and thought it would be more sensible for him not to dream or expect too much. But Nabil refused to live life without dreams! He loved drama and being mischievous, and he was never afraid to fight for something he believed in. His bones were as delicate as silk, but his will was as strong as iron.

When Nabil left the hospital, he lived in children's homes. As he grew up he sought out more and more adventures, navigating the world in his wheelchair and eventually setting off for university. Nabil soon realized there were very few opportunities for disabled actors and became determined to change this.

With a friend, Nabil set up the first ever inclusive theatre company. It was called Graeae, pronounced "gray eye." It was named after the Greek myth of three sisters who all shared one eye. Graeae is now world-famous and represents many actors of all talents and abilities. As the company blossomed, so did Nabil's acting career and he began appearing in films and TV shows such as *Doctor Who*. He has written plays and books and performed in productions for the National Theatre. He approaches everything he does as an activist, trying to make the world a better and more inclusive place.

Once, when Nabil was having a cup of tea in front of a huge poster of himself in a show, a man looked at Nabil's wheelchair, mistakenly thought he was begging and dropped money into Nabil's cup! Nabil just laughed. In this moment he showed amazing compassion, recognized that the man was ignorant, and decided he could forgive him. Nabil lives with his wife, Marcela, and their beloved dog Rainbow, who appeared one night on their doorstep and has not left Nabil's side since.

TERRY FOX

1958-1981 — Athlete

Not so long ago in the windswept Canadian city of Winnipeg, a boy was born named Terrance Stanley Fox. Terry's favorite thing was sport. He never wanted to lose a game of anything, so he practiced and practiced after school.

He excelled at football, baseball, rugby, and track and field, but it was basketball that held his heart. At five feet tall he was not an obvious choice for the team, but if he could play for just one minute, he felt it would be worth it. Through dedication, he did play for one magnificent minute in eighth grade. In twelfth grade, Terry won joint athlete of the year, with his best friend Doug.

Sport was everything to Terry and it framed all he did. After university he became a PE teacher. One winter's day Terry awoke with a pain in his knee—he tried to ignore it, but eventually went to the doctor. Terry was told he had cancer and would need to have his leg amputated and have chemotherapy. After this, he would have a 50 percent chance of living.

Terry was upset but determined to live. He learned that just two years earlier, people with the same form of cancer as him had only a 15 percent chance of survival. This increase to 50 percent was down to groundbreaking research done by scientists. He decided he would raise money to fund their amazing work.

Terry approached his recovery with characteristic energy. He joined a wheelchair basketball team while having chemotherapy and planned a "Marathon of Hope" across Canada. He aimed to raise one dollar from every Canadian.

Training for the marathon was hard: Terry's prosthetic leg meant he ran unevenly, which was painful. But in April 1980, Terry dipped his toes in the Atlantic Ocean in Newfoundland before beginning his epic run. He ran the equivalent of a marathon every single day. He faced raging gales, rain, and even snow. But his friend Doug drove alongside him and helped him keep going.

As news of his dream spread, Canadians flocked to support him. He was greeted by marching bands and sporting heroes, and raised huge amounts of money. By the time Terry reached Ontario, he was a superstar. But in Thunder Bay, after 143 days of marathons, Terry had to abandon the run. The cancer had spread to his lungs and he died nine months later, at just 22.

Terry's colossal efforts had not been in vain, and he left a huge legacy behind him. The annual Terry Fox Run is still a global event, and $750 million has been raised for cancer research in his name. His marathon was a true run of hope and the toughest sporting achievement of his life.

MARATHON
OF
HO

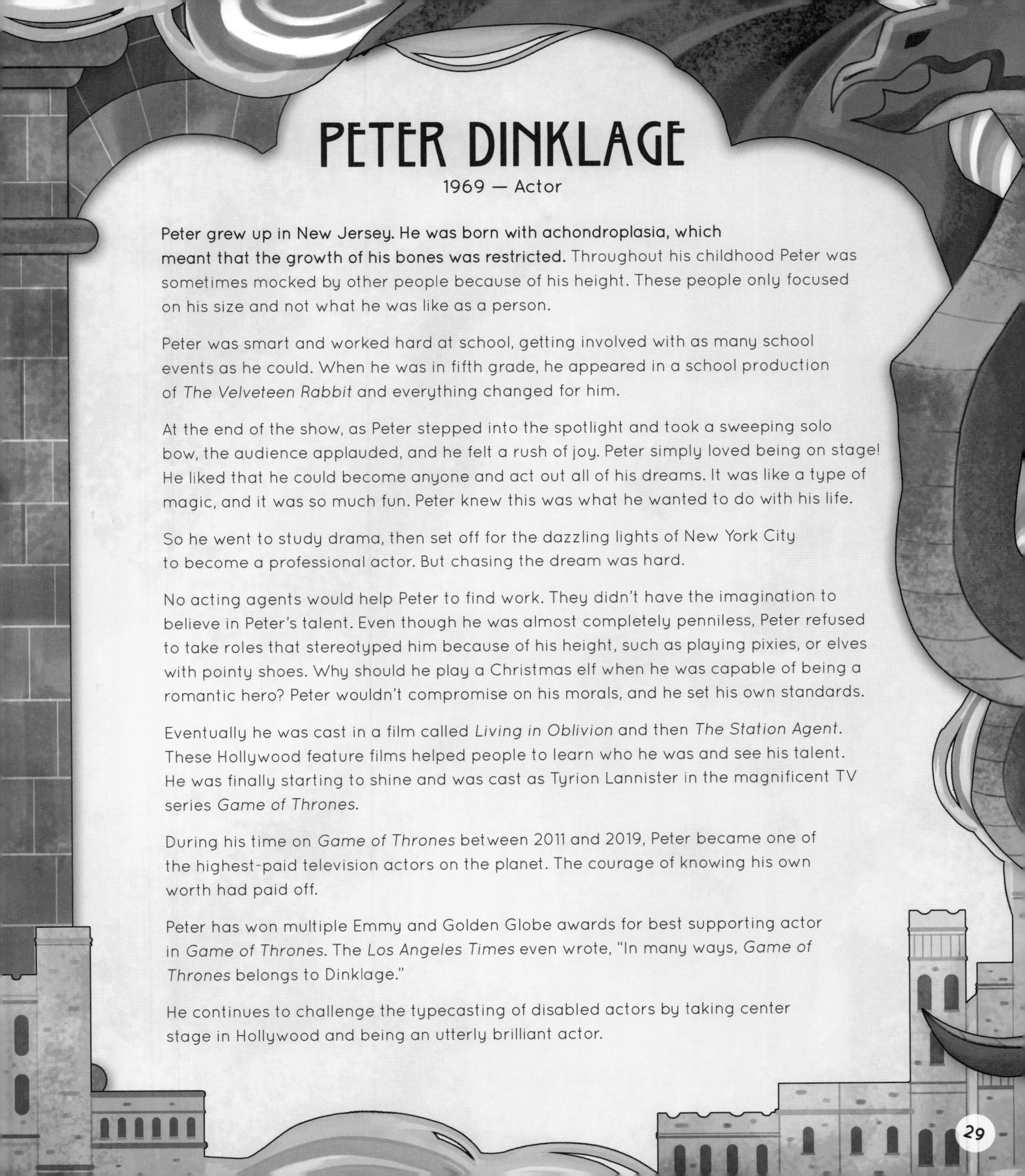

PETER DINKLAGE

1969 — Actor

Peter grew up in New Jersey. He was born with achondroplasia, which meant that the growth of his bones was restricted. Throughout his childhood Peter was sometimes mocked by other people because of his height. These people only focused on his size and not what he was like as a person.

Peter was smart and worked hard at school, getting involved with as many school events as he could. When he was in fifth grade, he appeared in a school production of *The Velveteen Rabbit* and everything changed for him.

At the end of the show, as Peter stepped into the spotlight and took a sweeping solo bow, the audience applauded, and he felt a rush of joy. Peter simply loved being on stage! He liked that he could become anyone and act out all of his dreams. It was like a type of magic, and it was so much fun. Peter knew this was what he wanted to do with his life.

So he went to study drama, then set off for the dazzling lights of New York City to become a professional actor. But chasing the dream was hard.

No acting agents would help Peter to find work. They didn't have the imagination to believe in Peter's talent. Even though he was almost completely penniless, Peter refused to take roles that stereotyped him because of his height, such as playing pixies, or elves with pointy shoes. Why should he play a Christmas elf when he was capable of being a romantic hero? Peter wouldn't compromise on his morals, and he set his own standards.

Eventually he was cast in a film called *Living in Oblivion* and then *The Station Agent*. These Hollywood feature films helped people to learn who he was and see his talent. He was finally starting to shine and was cast as Tyrion Lannister in the magnificent TV series *Game of Thrones*.

During his time on *Game of Thrones* between 2011 and 2019, Peter became one of the highest-paid television actors on the planet. The courage of knowing his own worth had paid off.

Peter has won multiple Emmy and Golden Globe awards for best supporting actor in *Game of Thrones*. The *Los Angeles Times* even wrote, "In many ways, *Game of Thrones* belongs to Dinklage."

He continues to challenge the typecasting of disabled actors by taking center stage in Hollywood and being an utterly brilliant actor.

Catalina Devandas

1972 — Lawyer

Catalina was a fiercely bright child. She grew up in the warm country of Costa Rica in Central America. Catalina had spina bifida, and used a wheelchair to help her move around.

She hated the pitying looks she sometimes got from people in her community. She felt especially frustrated when strangers would grab the handles of her wheelchair to push her, without asking permission.

"I can push myself!" she would fume.

As she grew older Catalina chose to ignore other people's ignorance. If someone doubted whether she could get married, have children, or pursue a marvelous career, she closed her mind to them and focused on her own dreams instead.

But it still troubled Catalina that because she used a wheelchair, her community had low expectations for her life. She soon realized that this narrow-mindedness wasn't unique to Costa Rica—it was a global problem.

Catalina was so fed up of abled people thinking that disabled people needed to be "cured," or that they were superheroes if they lived normal lives. She became determined to prove that disabled people have the same rights as everyone.

So, she took the handles off her wheelchair to stop people from pushing her! Then she got on with her life: she got married, had three children, and embarked upon an amazing career.

She studied to become a lawyer, working to get better rights for women. Then she became an advocate for disabled people all over the world, joining a huge and powerful organization called the United Nations. In 2004 an entirely new role within the UN was created just for Catalina: Special Rapporteur on the Rights of Persons with Disabilities.

Catalina has travelled to many countries, fighting for better rights for disabled people. She helped to write the Convention on the Rights of Persons with Disabilities, a document which is used all over the globe. It states that no one should be excluded due to their needs.

She is changing the world one government at a time, and firmly believes that "altering attitudes towards disabled people is a priority. You can start respecting us by listening to us."

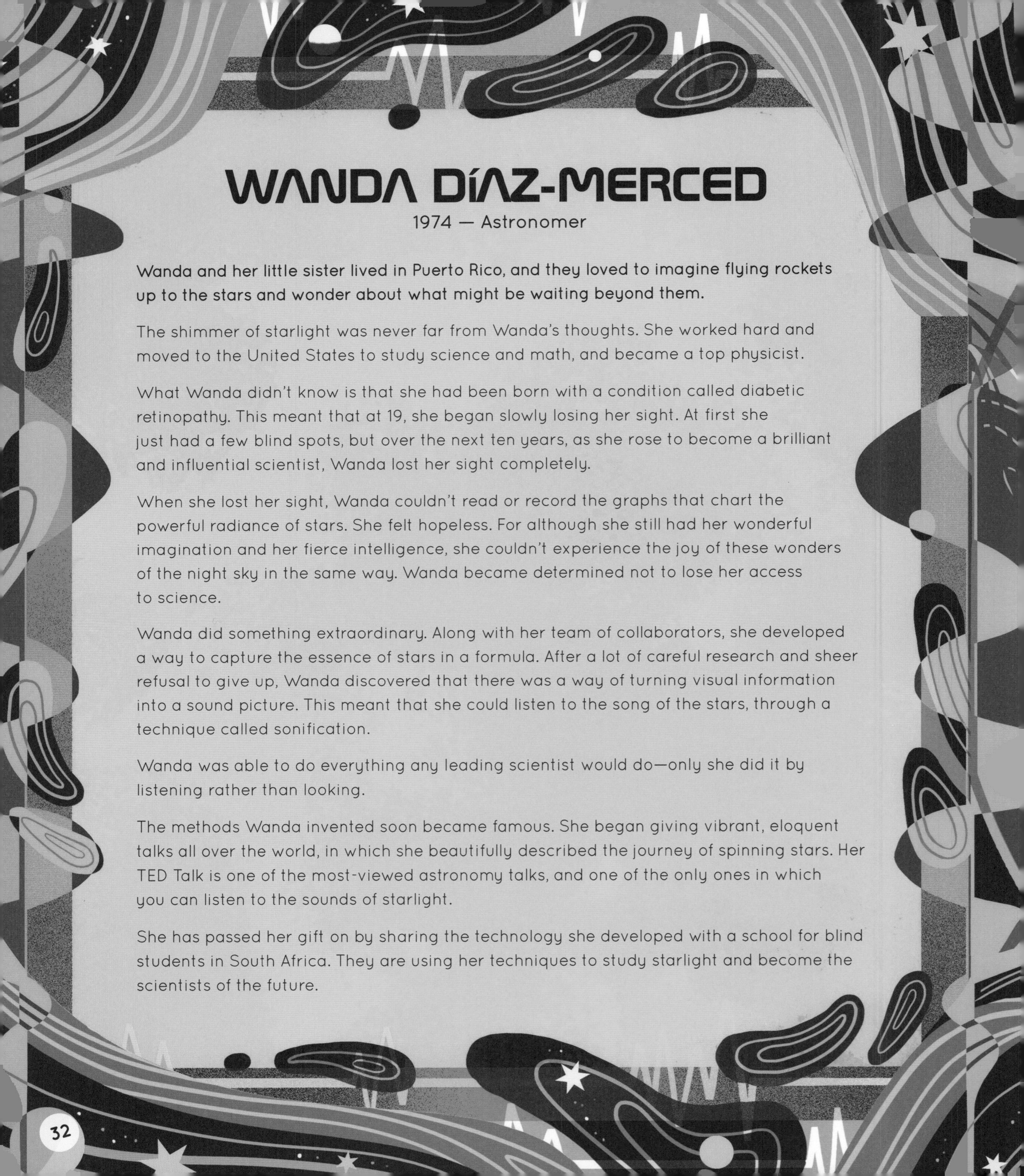

WANDA DÍAZ-MERCED

1974 — Astronomer

Wanda and her little sister lived in Puerto Rico, and they loved to imagine flying rockets up to the stars and wonder about what might be waiting beyond them.

The shimmer of starlight was never far from Wanda's thoughts. She worked hard and moved to the United States to study science and math, and became a top physicist.

What Wanda didn't know is that she had been born with a condition called diabetic retinopathy. This meant that at 19, she began slowly losing her sight. At first she just had a few blind spots, but over the next ten years, as she rose to become a brilliant and influential scientist, Wanda lost her sight completely.

When she lost her sight, Wanda couldn't read or record the graphs that chart the powerful radiance of stars. She felt hopeless. For although she still had her wonderful imagination and her fierce intelligence, she couldn't experience the joy of these wonders of the night sky in the same way. Wanda became determined not to lose her access to science.

Wanda did something extraordinary. Along with her team of collaborators, she developed a way to capture the essence of stars in a formula. After a lot of careful research and sheer refusal to give up, Wanda discovered that there was a way of turning visual information into a sound picture. This meant that she could listen to the song of the stars, through a technique called sonification.

Wanda was able to do everything any leading scientist would do—only she did it by listening rather than looking.

The methods Wanda invented soon became famous. She began giving vibrant, eloquent talks all over the world, in which she beautifully described the journey of spinning stars. Her TED Talk is one of the most-viewed astronomy talks, and one of the only ones in which you can listen to the sounds of starlight.

She has passed her gift on by sharing the technology she developed with a school for blind students in South Africa. They are using her techniques to study starlight and become the scientists of the future.

VICTOR PINEDA

1978 — Scholar and Activist

In 1978, in Venezuela, a boy named Victor was born. He was full of the spirit of adventure and dreamed of doing wonderful things.

When he was very young, Victor contracted polio. It weakened his muscles and made it hard for him to walk and even breathe. At seven, Victor started using a wheelchair to help him get around. By age 11 he needed a ventilator to help him breathe at night.

Victor was the same person, but the way people treated him changed. Not a single school that his mom took him to was prepared to teach him. Victor felt excluded and alone. But his family would not give up.

Victor and his family moved to the United States, where he found a school that welcomed him and a wonderful teacher, and he made plenty of friends. Victor's vivid dreams burned brighter, and he started to think about all the brilliant things he could do in the world.

When Victor reached his twenties, he needed the ventilator to breathe all the time, but he did not let this get in his way of what he wanted to do. In high school he discovered that he loved public speaking. He was chosen by his class as a commencement speaker at their graduation which was a very special honor.

Victor understood that the fact he had been originally deprived of an education was a denial of human rights. So, after graduating from Berkeley University, he set up the Pineda Foundation, which fights for the rights of young disabled people around the world.

Victor was determined to tell disabled people's stories in an honest, enlightening way. He started an online database of disabled people's histories called "It's Our Story," and launched *World Enabled* which is a positive source of information for young disabled people. As well as this, he helped create *Silver Scorpion*, a comic book about, and by, disabled children from Syria.

He now teaches at prestigious universities all over the world, educating people about how to build cities of the future that are accessible places created to support and enable everyone's dreams.

IT'S
OUR
STORY

ARUNIMA SINHA

1989 — Mountaineer and Explorer

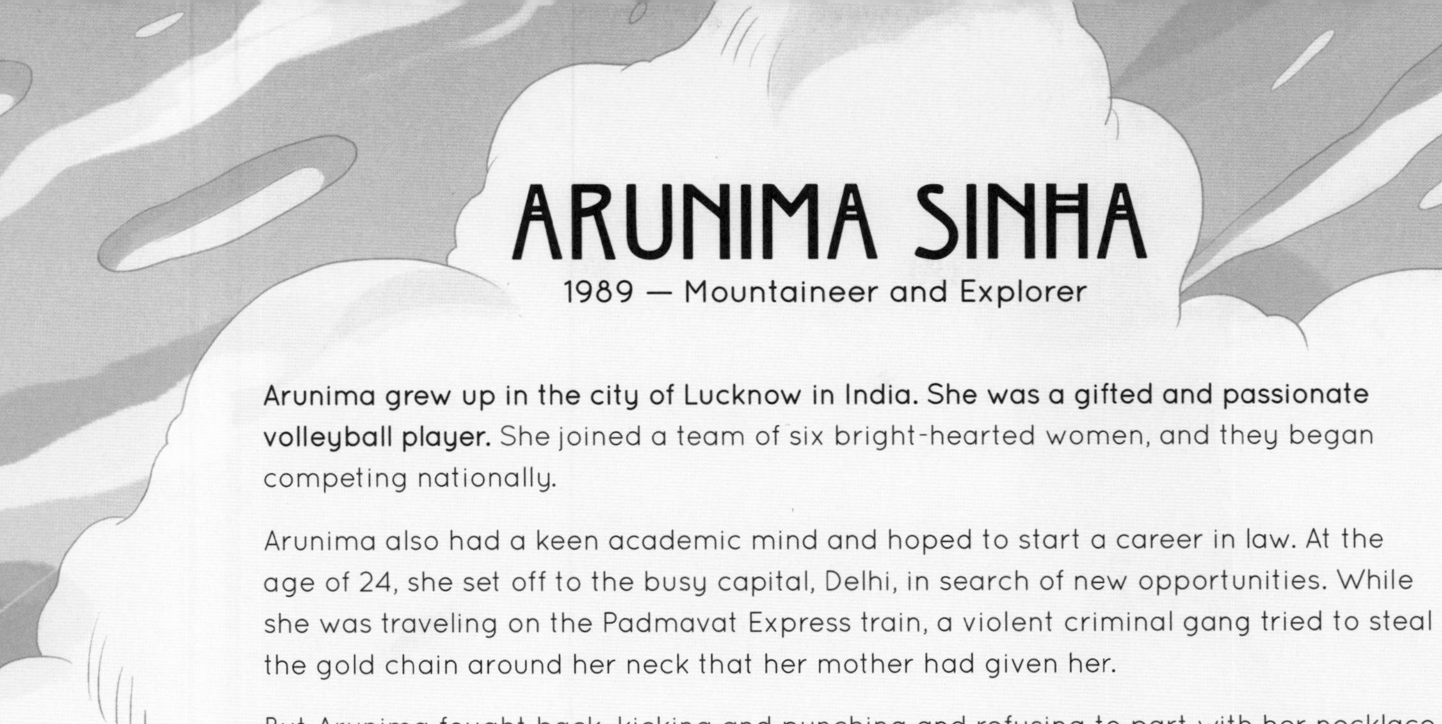

Arunima grew up in the city of Lucknow in India. She was a gifted and passionate volleyball player. She joined a team of six bright-hearted women, and they began competing nationally.

Arunima also had a keen academic mind and hoped to start a career in law. At the age of 24, she set off to the busy capital, Delhi, in search of new opportunities. While she was traveling on the Padmavat Express train, a violent criminal gang tried to steal the gold chain around her neck that her mother had given her.

But Arunima fought back, kicking and punching and refusing to part with her necklace. She was strong and fast, and when the gang realized they couldn't win, they pushed Arunima from the moving train.

Arunima lost the lower part of one of her legs in the attack, but escaped with her precious life. She spent all night shivering with shock on the railway track, but eventually she was found and taken to a hospital. Arunima spent four months in rehabilitation and, just two days after having a prosthetic leg fitted, she was walking again.

She knew she needed a challenge to keep her heart happy and body active, so she set herself a goal that would take her beyond the soaring clouds. She wanted to climb the seven highest mountain peaks in the world. She needed advice, so she approached a hero of hers: Bachendri Pal, who was the first Indian woman to climb Mount Everest.

They began training together, and despite the doubts of many around her, in 2013, after 18 months of physical challenge, Arunima became the first female amputee to reach the top of Mount Everest.

The climb was fraught with danger: at one point Arunima thought her oxygen supply might run out, but she kept going. Since 2013, she has climbed another six of the highest mountains in the world: Kilimanjaro in Tanzania, Elbrus in Russia, Kosciuszko in Australia, Aconcagua in Argentina, Carstensz Pyramid in Indonesia, and Mount Vinson in Antarctica.

She firmly believes that to climb a mountain, the thing you need most is a brave heart.

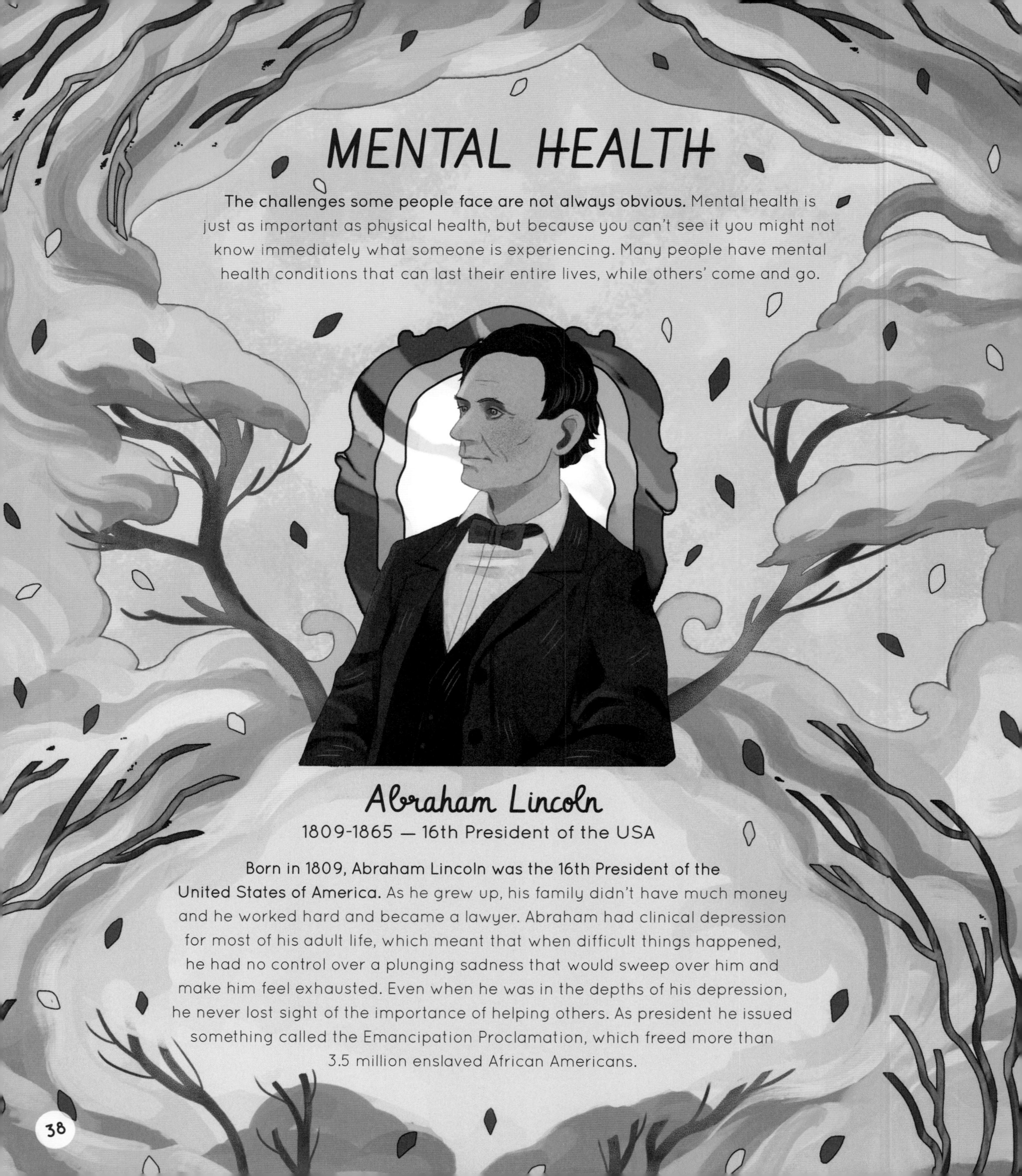

MENTAL HEALTH

The challenges some people face are not always obvious. Mental health is just as important as physical health, but because you can't see it you might not know immediately what someone is experiencing. Many people have mental health conditions that can last their entire lives, while others' come and go.

Abraham Lincoln

1809-1865 — 16th President of the USA

Born in 1809, Abraham Lincoln was the 16th President of the United States of America. As he grew up, his family didn't have much money and he worked hard and became a lawyer. Abraham had clinical depression for most of his adult life, which meant that when difficult things happened, he had no control over a plunging sadness that would sweep over him and make him feel exhausted. Even when he was in the depths of his depression, he never lost sight of the importance of helping others. As president he issued something called the Emancipation Proclamation, which freed more than 3.5 million enslaved African Americans.

Matt Haig

1975 — Author

Born in the north of England, Matt was quiet at school. He was teased because he loved reading and wearing bright yellow, and hated rugby.

As he got older, he started to feel an overwhelming sense of despair, experienced anxiety and depression, and felt he couldn't go on. Matt focused on taking each moment as it came, but it was frightening and required all his courage. He learned techniques to manage his anxiety in times of depression. Matt started to write about his condition and turned his experiences into perceptive, witty, and useful books. His memoir *Reasons to Stay Alive* was a number one bestseller.

He lives in Brighton, England, with his wife and children, still wears yellow, hates rugby, and loves books. Matt says that mental health is physical health. To think of the two things as separate is highly damaging. There is only health.

Demi Lovato

1992 — Singer-songwriter

In sunny Texas, there once was a girl named Demi who loved to sing and dance. She starred in a show called *Barney and Friends*. But Demi was bullied because of her success and so her family homeschooled her. Demi went on to become an award-winning pop star. She worked hard, but she was still in the middle of growing up and discovering who she was. She became depressed, developed bulimia, and started to self-harm, which seemed to help her feel in control. Soon she became dependent on alcohol to numb her feelings of anxiety and sadness. By 18, she felt so hopeless and burned out, Demi thought it might be better if she ended her life. Thankfully, with her family and friends supporting her, she dedicated time to recovering and sought proper help. She is now sober and living a much healthier life, being kinder to herself and valuing self-care over self-sabotage.

NO
EXCUSES
NO
LIMITS

REDOUAN AIT CHITT

1989 — Breakdancer

Once, in a small town in Holland, a baby boy named Redo was born. Redo had many differences compared to other babies. One of his hips was missing a bone, one of his arms was short, he had five fingers in total, and one leg was shorter than the other.

The doctors peered at Redo with confused faces. As he grew up the doctors gave him equipment he found embarrassing, such as a yellow tricycle which Redo hated. His family felt that these things weren't helping their child and were determined to do things their own way. A way that showed him life was full of possibilities.

So they bought Redo a cool green mountain bike, took him to the top of a hill, and let him soar down it. Redo felt the wind whip through his hair, saw the world rush past him, and, of course, crashed at the bottom. He didn't care how many times he fell—riding the bike felt like freedom!

Riding his green bike was amazing, but Redo still felt judged. Everywhere he went, children whispered, pointed, and stared at him. He dreamed of being famous so that people would just accept him.

When he was 14, Redo saw a group of break-dancers at his school and it set his soul on fire. He longed to jump and dive and spin, like they did.

With a gang of loyal friends, Redo joined a dance class. He didn't know if he would be able to keep up. Before they began, the teacher said, "Breaking is all about being yourself and finding your identity through movement." And Redo knew his individuality could be his talent.

He loved breaking and the uplifting culture around it, which celebrated being unique. But it was not easy! Just like when he had learned to ride his green bike, Redo kept falling down. He practiced every day after school. He got hurt, picked himself up, and tried again.

Through his creativity, grit, and perseverance, he became a dazzling dancer. People gasped when they saw Redo twirl upside down or scoot across the floor on his elbow. He had not just become a fearless breaker, but a gifted choreographer.

Redo began competing all over the world, set up his own dance school, and joined a crew of some of the best disabled breakers on the planet. Performing is his life and he uses his body in a powerful, positive way, which gives him a sense of freedom that feels as good as flying.

EMMANUEL OFOSU YEBOAH

1977 — Athlete

On New Year's Day in 1977 a little boy was born in Ghana, and his parents called him Emmanuel. He had been born with no shinbone in his right leg, making it difficult for him to walk. He lived in a place where disability was misunderstood and incorrectly thought to be a curse. His father believed this and left the family home.

The community urged Emmanuel's mother, a wonderful woman named Comfort, to abandon her baby too, but she loved her little boy with all her heart and knew that his life was of no less value just because he was physically different. As Emmanuel grew, Comfort encouraged him and raised him to believe he could do anything.

Emmanuel lived in a poor village and his home had neither electricity nor a proper bed, but it was full of love, hope, and happiness. Comfort was determined for her boy to go to school, so she carried him two miles there and two miles back each day.

Soon Emmanuel grew too big to be carried, so he hopped all the way to school. When he graduated, he went off to work in the capital city, Accra. For the first time he saw other disabled people. But most of them had been deprived of education and were forced to beg on the streets. Emmanuel knew he must do something to change things.

Emmanuel decided he would cycle around Ghana to raise awareness for the rights of disabled people. He sat down and wrote the first letter he had ever written. In it he asked for a grant for a bicycle. He was successful, but he needed more support. So, he gathered his courage and went to the King of Ghana! Disabled people were not allowed in the palace, but Emmanuel didn't give up, and the king finally agreed to see him.

The king saw Emmanuel's plan was important and offered to endorse his journey. In 2001, at the age of 24, Emmanuel set off on his bike, proving that with determination, support and the right equipment, anyone can succeed. He became well-known and loved in Ghana. He was able to have surgery and chose to have a prosthetic leg so he could walk without crutches and cycle faster.

He was a torchbearer for Ghana in the 2004 Olympics and has set up many charities to improve the lives of the disabled community in Ghana. He firmly believes that if you have a dream, you should never give up.

FARIDA BEDWEI

1979 — Software Engineer

In the sunny city of Lagos in Nigeria lived a little girl named Farida. Just after her first birthday, Farida's family found out she had been born with a condition called cerebral palsy. Her parents were dynamic and traveled the world with their family, doing important work. They loved their daughter and were not fazed by the condition, because they knew she was fiercely bright and capable.

As Farida's family moved between the Caribbean and the UK, they educated her at home. As she traveled, Farida experienced many different attitudes towards her cerebral palsy: sometimes people were kind to her, sometimes they were dismissive, and sometimes they were just plain rude.

Farida was constantly faced with challenges, such as tackling the stairs, exploring big cities with poor accessibility, or crossing new terrain. It was important to her to think fast and fight to find new solutions, before anyone had time to doubt her.

When Farida was nine, her family moved to Ghana, and at age 12 she went to a mainstream school for the first time. Farida immediately developed a passion for computers and technology. She was so talented that she was accepted into a computer course. This meant that she skipped high school and went straight into higher education. She was the youngest person taking the course.

When the course finished, Farida applied for her dream job with a software company, telling them that although she didn't have experience, she was inspired to learn. They loved her boldness and gave her a job.

As Farida's career took off, she went on to run her own company. Running a company as a disabled woman in Ghana was not easy. But she was not put off by challenges, and the thing she loved about technology was that she could create brilliant software for people without meeting them in person, which meant that she could work without anyone judging her as a disabled person.

Keen to spread a positive message and challenge perceptions far and wide, Farida created a comic book superhero named Karmzah, who has cerebral palsy and magical crutches that give her power. She performs awesome stunts, fights villains, and is fearless in all she does—and just like her author, she doesn't let things stand in her way.

PARALYMPIC STARS

Since 1960, disabled athletes from around the world at the top of their game have participated in the Paralympic Games. Every four years, these great athletes challenge perceptions of disabled people as they achieve glory.

Jonas Jacobsson

1965 — Sport Shooter

Jonas Jacobsson grew up in Sweden. He had a lower limb impairment so he used a wheelchair to get around. As a young adult he developed a talent for sport shooting. He had a brilliant eye and incredible aim: he would get into position in his chair and fire his rifle, never missing a shot. His gift took him to one of the first Paralympics ever held, hosted by both Stoke Mandeville in the UK and New York in the USA.

Jonas has competed in nine Summer Paralympics and won 17 gold, two silver, and nine bronze medals. In 2008 Jonas became the first Paralympic athlete to be awarded Sweden's highest medal of sporting achievement: the Svenska Dagbladet Gold Medal.

Trischa Zorn

1964 — Swimmer

California golden girl Trischa Zorn was born blind. As a young girl she developed a love of water and found power in swimming. Trischa studied at the University of Nebraska, and when she wasn't studying she swam and trained hard, becoming fast and fearless in the pool. She has some vision, and is able to use the black line at the bottom of the pool to guide her.

She has competed in 7 Paralympic Games, and is the biggest superstar in the Games' history, having won 55 medals—41 gold, five silver and nine bronze.

Ade Adepitan

1973 — Wheelchair Basketball Player and TV Presenter

Nigerian-born Ade Adepitan moved to east London, England, with his family when he was three. Ade contracted polio as a baby and grew up using leg calipers to help him walk. But the calipers didn't help him much, and Ade found independence playing soccer with his friends, catching a ride on the back of a bike, or tearing about in a shopping cart. As a teen Ade was spotted by a wheelchair basketball coach, but he was unsure about using a wheelchair. Eventually, after some convincing, he gave it a go.

The freedom Ade felt from being able to move around so quickly and freely was fantastic, but he had to become an amazing wheelchair basketball player. Ade has represented Great Britain many times, helping lead his team to glory by winning Bronze at the 2004 Paralympics in Athens, and Gold at the 2005 Paralympic World Cup in Manchester, England. He is a much-loved TV presenter, travel journalist, children's author, and national treasure.

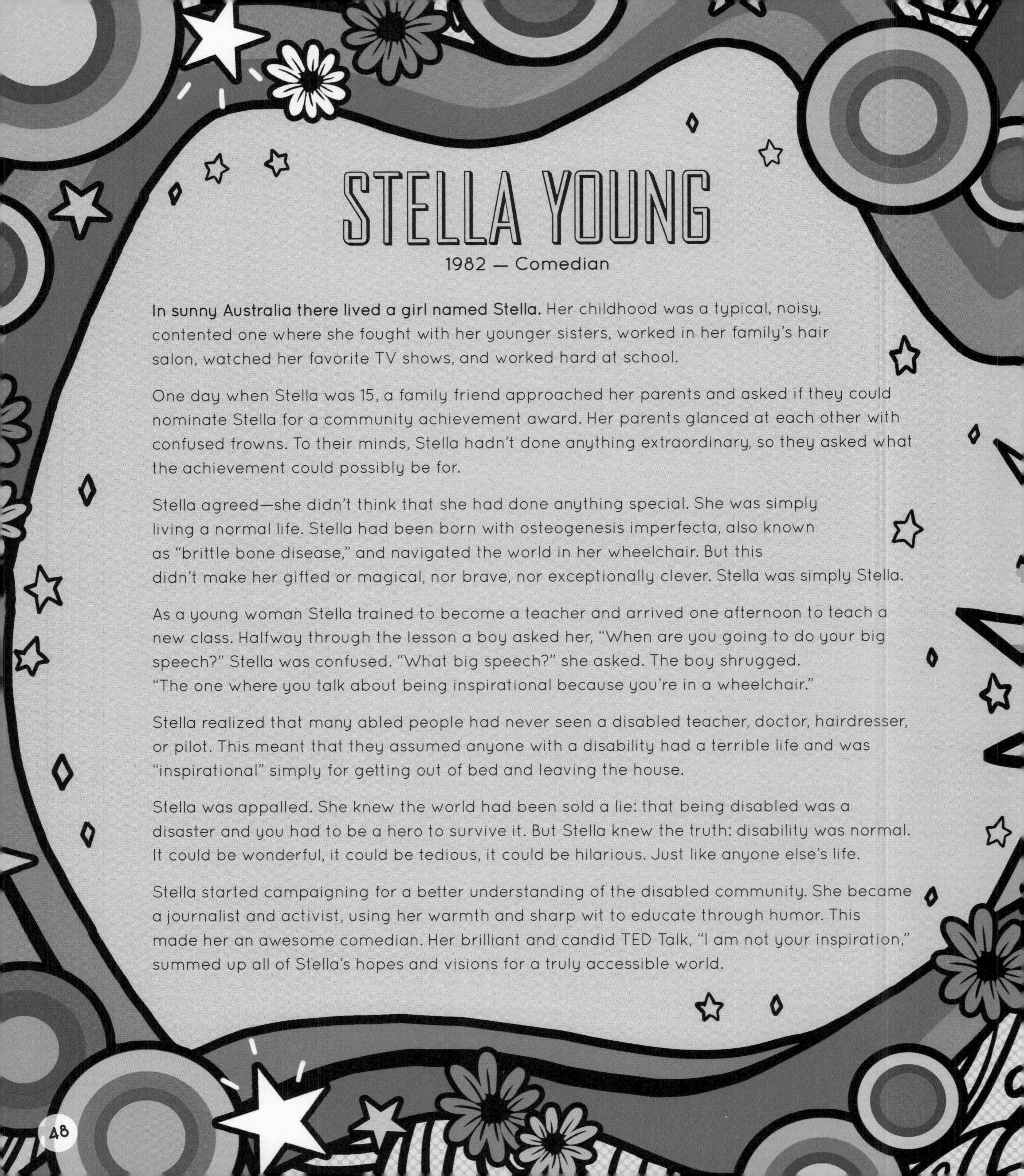

STELLA YOUNG

1982 — Comedian

In sunny Australia there lived a girl named Stella. Her childhood was a typical, noisy, contented one where she fought with her younger sisters, worked in her family's hair salon, watched her favorite TV shows, and worked hard at school.

One day when Stella was 15, a family friend approached her parents and asked if they could nominate Stella for a community achievement award. Her parents glanced at each other with confused frowns. To their minds, Stella hadn't done anything extraordinary, so they asked what the achievement could possibly be for.

Stella agreed—she didn't think that she had done anything special. She was simply living a normal life. Stella had been born with osteogenesis imperfecta, also known as "brittle bone disease," and navigated the world in her wheelchair. But this didn't make her gifted or magical, nor brave, nor exceptionally clever. Stella was simply Stella.

As a young woman Stella trained to become a teacher and arrived one afternoon to teach a new class. Halfway through the lesson a boy asked her, "When are you going to do your big speech?" Stella was confused. "What big speech?" she asked. The boy shrugged. "The one where you talk about being inspirational because you're in a wheelchair."

Stella realized that many abled people had never seen a disabled teacher, doctor, hairdresser, or pilot. This meant that they assumed anyone with a disability had a terrible life and was "inspirational" simply for getting out of bed and leaving the house.

Stella was appalled. She knew the world had been sold a lie: that being disabled was a disaster and you had to be a hero to survive it. But Stella knew the truth: disability was normal. It could be wonderful, it could be tedious, it could be hilarious. Just like anyone else's life.

Stella started campaigning for a better understanding of the disabled community. She became a journalist and activist, using her warmth and sharp wit to educate through humor. This made her an awesome comedian. Her brilliant and candid TED Talk, "I am not your inspiration," summed up all of Stella's hopes and visions for a truly accessible world.

I am not your inspiration

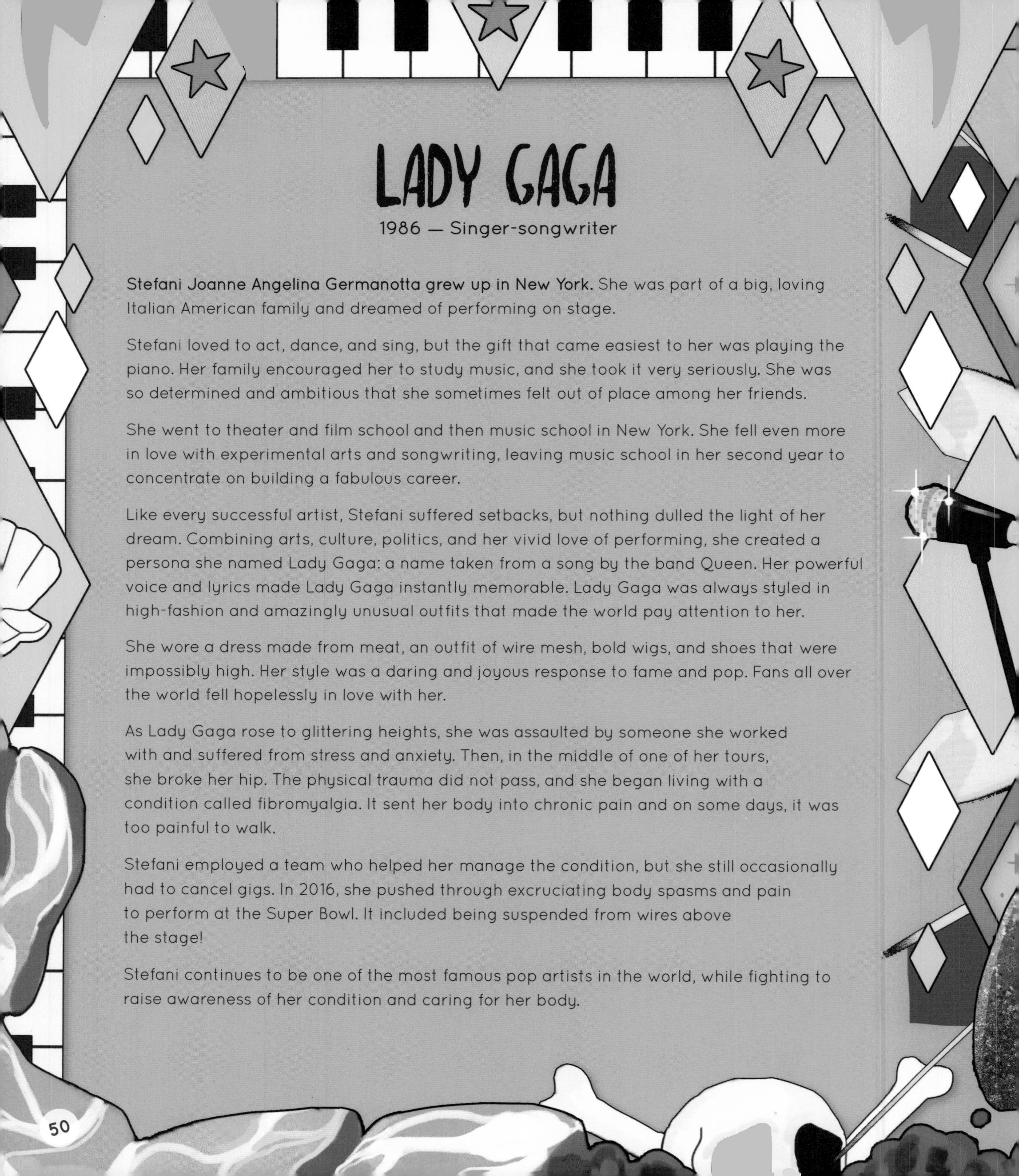

LADY GAGA

1986 — Singer-songwriter

Stefani Joanne Angelina Germanotta grew up in New York. She was part of a big, loving Italian American family and dreamed of performing on stage.

Stefani loved to act, dance, and sing, but the gift that came easiest to her was playing the piano. Her family encouraged her to study music, and she took it very seriously. She was so determined and ambitious that she sometimes felt out of place among her friends.

She went to theater and film school and then music school in New York. She fell even more in love with experimental arts and songwriting, leaving music school in her second year to concentrate on building a fabulous career.

Like every successful artist, Stefani suffered setbacks, but nothing dulled the light of her dream. Combining arts, culture, politics, and her vivid love of performing, she created a persona she named Lady Gaga: a name taken from a song by the band Queen. Her powerful voice and lyrics made Lady Gaga instantly memorable. Lady Gaga was always styled in high-fashion and amazingly unusual outfits that made the world pay attention to her.

She wore a dress made from meat, an outfit of wire mesh, bold wigs, and shoes that were impossibly high. Her style was a daring and joyous response to fame and pop. Fans all over the world fell hopelessly in love with her.

As Lady Gaga rose to glittering heights, she was assaulted by someone she worked with and suffered from stress and anxiety. Then, in the middle of one of her tours, she broke her hip. The physical trauma did not pass, and she began living with a condition called fibromyalgia. It sent her body into chronic pain and on some days, it was too painful to walk.

Stefani employed a team who helped her manage the condition, but she still occasionally had to cancel gigs. In 2016, she pushed through excruciating body spasms and pain to perform at the Super Bowl. It included being suspended from wires above the stage!

Stefani continues to be one of the most famous pop artists in the world, while fighting to raise awareness of her condition and caring for her body.

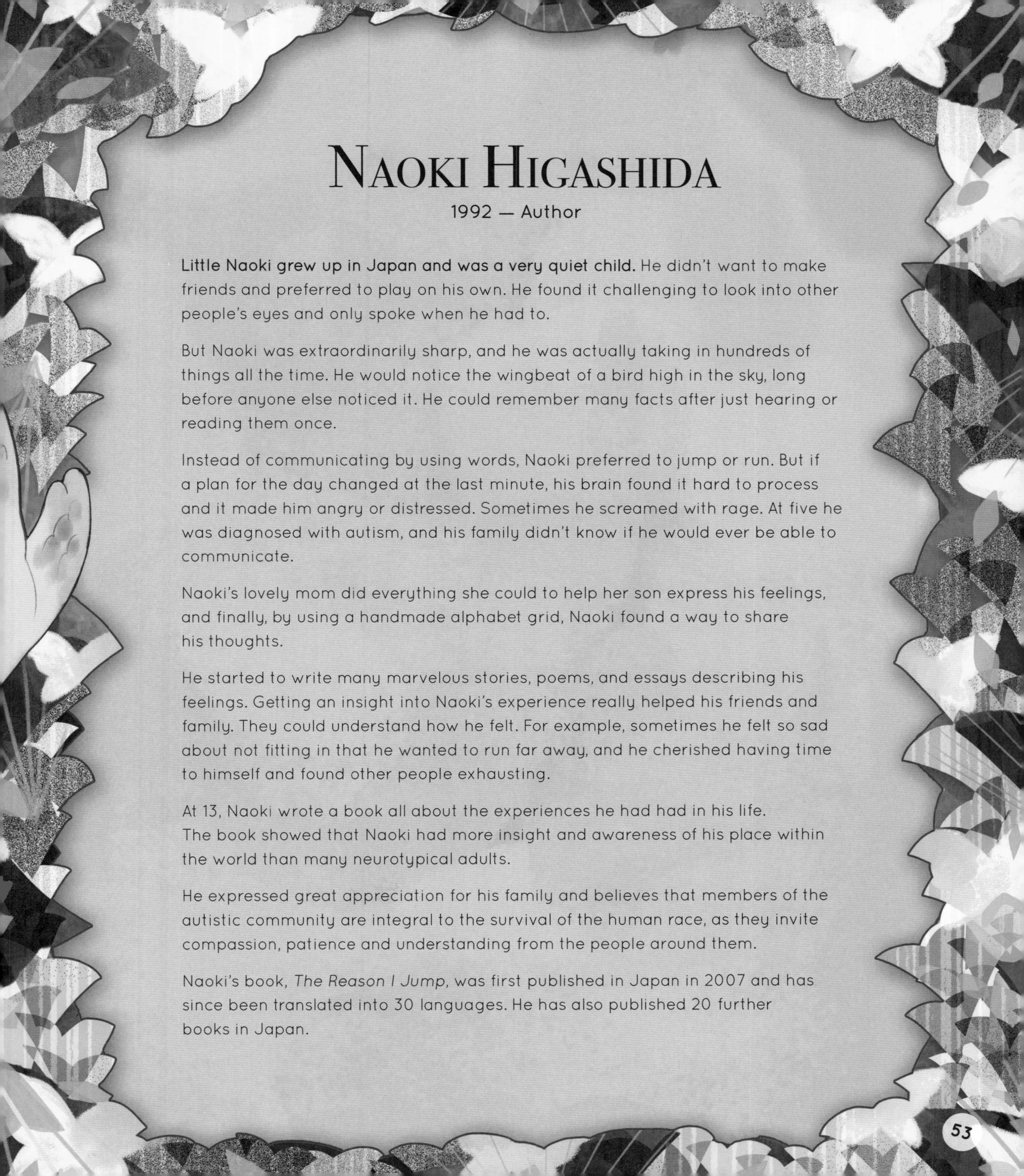

Naoki Higashida

1992 — Author

Little Naoki grew up in Japan and was a very quiet child. He didn't want to make friends and preferred to play on his own. He found it challenging to look into other people's eyes and only spoke when he had to.

But Naoki was extraordinarily sharp, and he was actually taking in hundreds of things all the time. He would notice the wingbeat of a bird high in the sky, long before anyone else noticed it. He could remember many facts after just hearing or reading them once.

Instead of communicating by using words, Naoki preferred to jump or run. But if a plan for the day changed at the last minute, his brain found it hard to process and it made him angry or distressed. Sometimes he screamed with rage. At five he was diagnosed with autism, and his family didn't know if he would ever be able to communicate.

Naoki's lovely mom did everything she could to help her son express his feelings, and finally, by using a handmade alphabet grid, Naoki found a way to share his thoughts.

He started to write many marvelous stories, poems, and essays describing his feelings. Getting an insight into Naoki's experience really helped his friends and family. They could understand how he felt. For example, sometimes he felt so sad about not fitting in that he wanted to run far away, and he cherished having time to himself and found other people exhausting.

At 13, Naoki wrote a book all about the experiences he had had in his life. The book showed that Naoki had more insight and awareness of his place within the world than many neurotypical adults.

He expressed great appreciation for his family and believes that members of the autistic community are integral to the survival of the human race, as they invite compassion, patience and understanding from the people around them.

Naoki's book, *The Reason I Jump*, was first published in Japan in 2007 and has since been translated into 30 languages. He has also published 20 further books in Japan.

Isabella Springmuhl Tejada

1997 — Designer

There once was a little girl from Guatemala named Isabella. She had four older siblings and a fabulous grandmother who was a designer. At only six years old, Isabella started sewing clothes and styling outfits for her dolls. Her family noticed that she had a real eye for detail. They lovingly gave her the nickname Belita, which means "little beauty" in Spanish.

Isabella was drawn to bright fabrics and Guatemalan folk-style embroidery. As she got older, her love of fabric and fairy tales blossomed and she created beautiful clothes filled with the colors, wonder, and tradition of her culture.

Once Isabella had graduated from college with a degree in science, she applied to study fashion. Even though Isabella's designs were unique and exquisitely made, she was rejected from fashion school because she had Down Syndrome.

But Isabella did not give up hope. She had been sketching and stitching dresses since she was young. She felt inspired by vivid tones, flowing scarves, and knitted ponchos. She wanted to keep creating clothes that she would love herself.

Isabella discovered that there were no other designers with Down Syndrome and no clothes being designed to suit her body type. She knew in her heart she had to fight to change this. Isabella designed bright, glorious clothes that she was proud to wear.

Supported by her family, Isabella set up her own incredible fashion label called DOWN TO XJABELLE, with a mission to "design beautiful and fashionable clothing for young people and adults with Down Syndrome."

Isabella's success soon spread. At age 19 she became the first person with Down Syndrome to showcase her collection at London Fashion Week, modeling some of the looks herself. Her designs featured Mayan textiles and traditional knitting with modern shapes and cutting-edge patterns. When asked about her mission, Isabella replied, "I believe that together we can knit a better world."

Isabella's star continues to rise in the fashion industry. She continues to push for inclusion, celebrate difference, and bring color to the world.

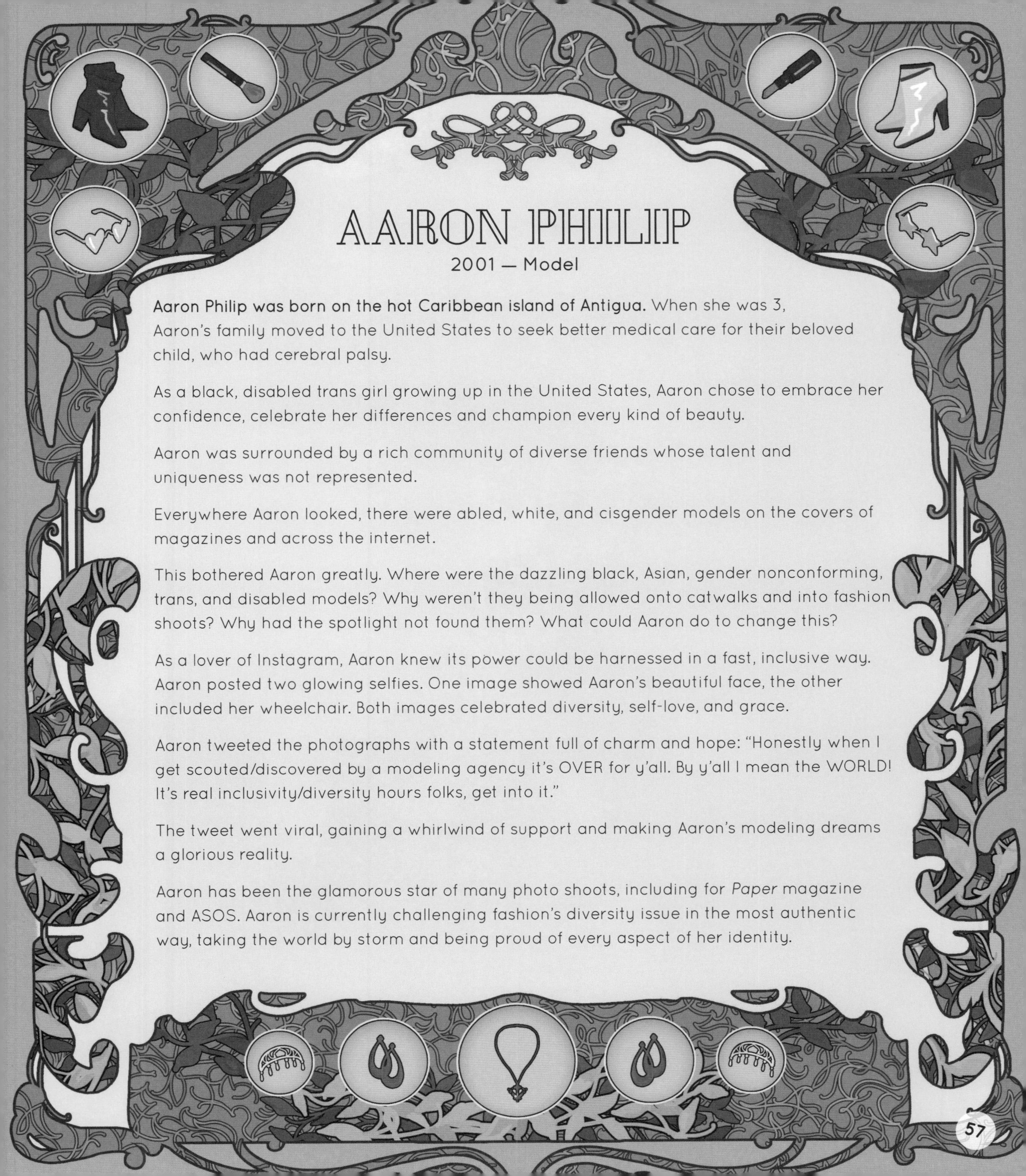

AARON PHILIP

2001 — Model

Aaron Philip was born on the hot Caribbean island of Antigua. When she was 3, Aaron's family moved to the United States to seek better medical care for their beloved child, who had cerebral palsy.

As a black, disabled trans girl growing up in the United States, Aaron chose to embrace her confidence, celebrate her differences and champion every kind of beauty.

Aaron was surrounded by a rich community of diverse friends whose talent and uniqueness was not represented.

Everywhere Aaron looked, there were abled, white, and cisgender models on the covers of magazines and across the internet.

This bothered Aaron greatly. Where were the dazzling black, Asian, gender nonconforming, trans, and disabled models? Why weren't they being allowed onto catwalks and into fashion shoots? Why had the spotlight not found them? What could Aaron do to change this?

As a lover of Instagram, Aaron knew its power could be harnessed in a fast, inclusive way. Aaron posted two glowing selfies. One image showed Aaron's beautiful face, the other included her wheelchair. Both images celebrated diversity, self-love, and grace.

Aaron tweeted the photographs with a statement full of charm and hope: "Honestly when I get scouted/discovered by a modeling agency it's OVER for y'all. By y'all I mean the WORLD! It's real inclusivity/diversity hours folks, get into it."

The tweet went viral, gaining a whirlwind of support and making Aaron's modeling dreams a glorious reality.

Aaron has been the glamorous star of many photo shoots, including for *Paper* magazine and ASOS. Aaron is currently challenging fashion's diversity issue in the most authentic way, taking the world by storm and being proud of every aspect of her identity.

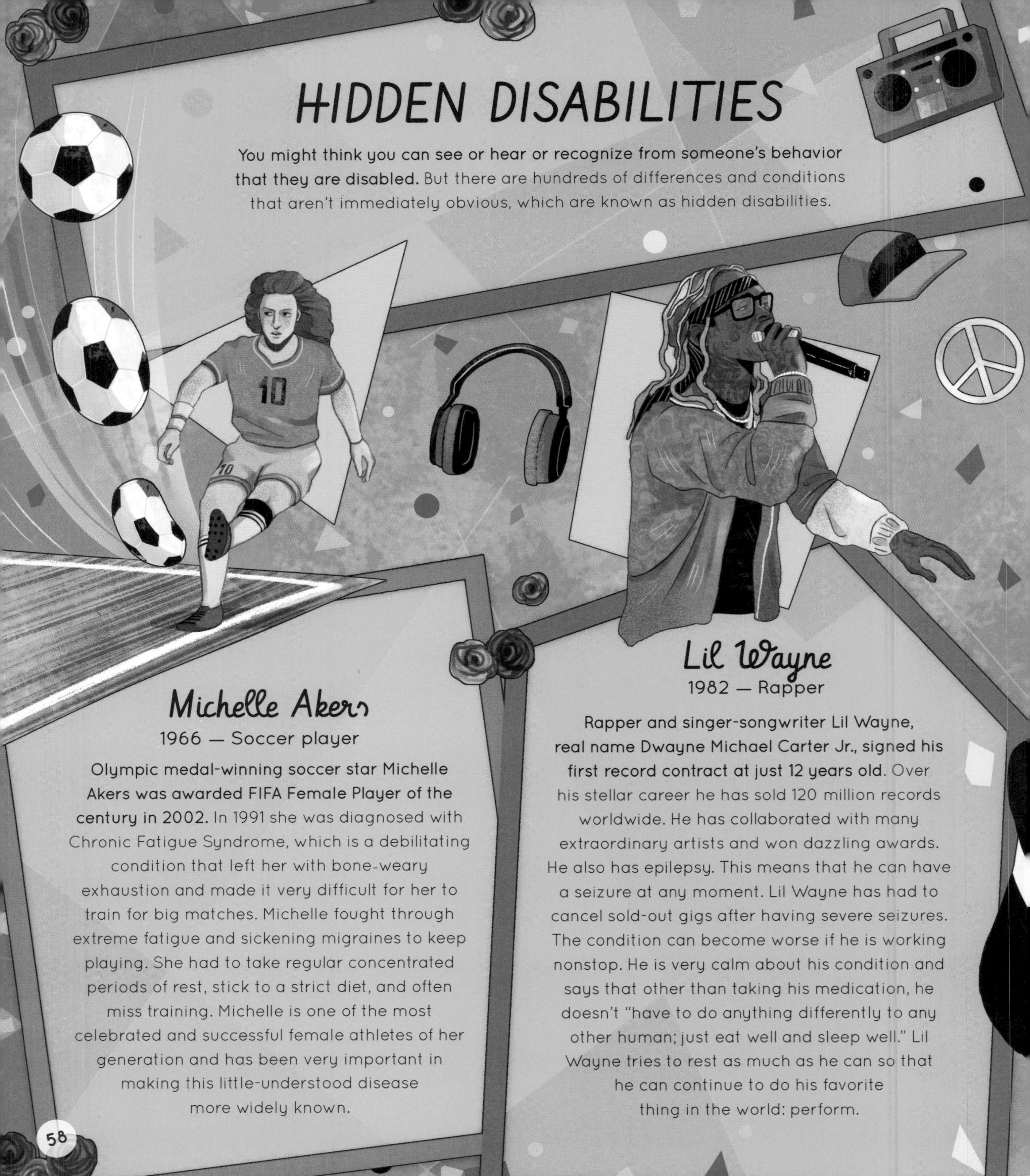

HIDDEN DISABILITIES

You might think you can see or hear or recognize from someone's behavior that they are disabled. But there are hundreds of differences and conditions that aren't immediately obvious, which are known as hidden disabilities.

Michelle Akers

1966 — Soccer player

Olympic medal-winning soccer star Michelle Akers was awarded FIFA Female Player of the century in 2002. In 1991 she was diagnosed with Chronic Fatigue Syndrome, which is a debilitating condition that left her with bone-weary exhaustion and made it very difficult for her to train for big matches. Michelle fought through extreme fatigue and sickening migraines to keep playing. She had to take regular concentrated periods of rest, stick to a strict diet, and often miss training. Michelle is one of the most celebrated and successful female athletes of her generation and has been very important in making this little-understood disease more widely known.

Lil Wayne

1982 — Rapper

Rapper and singer-songwriter Lil Wayne, real name Dwayne Michael Carter Jr., signed his first record contract at just 12 years old. Over his stellar career he has sold 120 million records worldwide. He has collaborated with many extraordinary artists and won dazzling awards. He also has epilepsy. This means that he can have a seizure at any moment. Lil Wayne has had to cancel sold-out gigs after having severe seizures. The condition can become worse if he is working nonstop. He is very calm about his condition and says that other than taking his medication, he doesn't "have to do anything differently to any other human; just eat well and sleep well." Lil Wayne tries to rest as much as he can so that he can continue to do his favorite thing in the world: perform.

Dynamo

1982 — Magician

Steven Frayne, better known as Dynamo, is a spectacular magician from Bradford, England. His grandpa taught him his first ever magic trick to help show bullies not to mess with him! It worked, and Dynamo has never stopped performing magic since. His most famous tricks include walking across the surface of the River Thames, levitating beside a London bus as it drove through the city, and making people mysteriously vanish into thin air. Alongside his dazzling career Dynamo has been diagnosed with Crohn's disease, which is a serious long-term condition that affects the digestive system and can flare up at any point. When it does flare up, he has to take medication, which alters his appearance and has other side effects. He has spoken very openly and honestly about how he manages the condition alongside his career as a magician. He continues to wow fans and take people's breath away with his spellbinding tricks.

GLOSSARY TERMS

ACHONDROPLASIA An inherited condition that affects bone growth. People with the condition are short in stature, with limbs that are short in proportion to their body length.

ACTIVIST Someone who campaigns to bring about political or social change.

AMERICAN CIVIL LIBERTIES UNION An organization defending and protecting the constitutional rights of United States citizens.

APPENDICITIS A painful swelling of the appendix, resolved by an operation to remove it. Without treatment, the appendix can burst.

AUTISM A broad-ranging condition affecting people in different ways. A brain divergence that influences the way people see the world and communicate. It falls under the umbrella of neurodiversity.

BLACK HOLE Usually created by the collapse of a massive star, a black hole has a gravitational field so strong that no light or matter can escape it.

BULIMIA An eating disorder and mental health condition. Someone with bulimia repeats the behavior of eating a large amount of food in a short space of time (binge eating), and then trying to get rid of the food (purging) by making themselves sick, taking medicine to make them go to the toilet, fasting, or doing extreme and excessive exercise.

CANCER A condition where cells grow and multiply uncontrollably. The cancerous cells can damage and destroy healthy cells, tissue, and organs.

CHEMOTHERAPY A medical treatment for cancer that aims to kill off fast-growing cancerous cells, but that also has an impact on healthy cells.

CHOREOGRAPHER Someone who creates dance routines.

CHRONIC Something that continues for a long time, or comes back regularly.

CISGENDER Someone whose gender identity is aligned with the sex that they were assigned at birth.

CLINICAL DEPRESSION An ongoing period of low mood, and a lack of interest in usual activities, that lasts for most of the day and continues for more than two weeks.

COMPOSER A person who writes pieces of music.

CROHN'S DISEASE A condition where part of the digestive system is inflamed and painful, leading to abdominal pain, diarrhea, and tiredness.

DIABETIC RETINOPATHY A complication of diabetes that can lead to blindness. The high blood-sugar levels that can occur with diabetes can damage the blood vessels in the eye.

EPILEPSY A condition that affects the brain, leading to seizures. These are bursts of electrical activity that affect how the brain works for a short time.

FIBROMYALGIA A long-term condition involving pain spread through various parts of the body and extreme tiredness.

GOVERNESS Someone employed to teach children at their home.

IDENTITY Who someone is and how they think about themselves. The qualities, beliefs and characteristics that make someone who they are.

IDENTITY-FIRST LANGUAGE Placing someone's disability first in a phrase. Some (but not all) people prefer this as they consider their disability an important part of who they are.

INCUBATOR A rigid container which keeps the temperature and environment stable for a baby.

JOURNALIST Someone who puts together information as stories either in written form or to be broadcast on radio or television.

LEG CALIPER A brace that provides support to the leg and can be used to hold it in a certain position.

CHRONIC FATIGUE SYNDROME A condition that causes extreme tiredness, but can also have other effects such as headaches, muscle and joint pain and dizziness and nausea.

MIGRAINE An intense, throbbing headache. Often includes a sensitivity to light and sounds, and feeling sick.

MOTOR NEURON DISEASE A condition where messages from the brain stop reaching the muscles.

NEUROTYPICAL Meaning neurologically typical, and expressing how society generally expects people's brains to function. The opposite is neurodiverse, which is a term used to describe brains that are wired in a different way from this, such as those of people with autism, ADHD, or dyslexia, among others.

OSTEOGENESIS IMPERFECTA A condition that affects the bones, causing them to break easily. The severity of the condition varies and can lead to short stature, breathing problems, and hearing loss.

OSTEOMALACIA A condition where someone's bones don't form the hard coating needed to keep them strong. The bones remain soft, which can make them more likely to bend or crack. This can be very painful.

POLIO An infection that in some cases affects the nerves in the spine and brain, causing paralysis in the legs. This usually wears off, but can have long-term effects.

PREACHER A person who delivers a religious sermon, often as their job.

PROSTHETIC A manufactured body part, such as a leg, hand, or arm, that is used to replace a part that is considered missing.

RACISM The belief that some races are better than others and treating a person or people differently based on their race.

REHABILITATION A program or various therapies to help someone recover from injury or illness.

SEIZURE Bursts of electrical activity that affect how the brain works for a short time. These can cause convulsions and usually happen to someone with epilepsy.

SLAVERY A situation where people are owned by others, or held under their complete control, with no ability to leave. They are forced to obey and treated as objects that can be bought, sold, and exploited.

SONIFICATION Uses data in a standardized way to create sound signals that convey information.

SPEECH THERAPY Supporting those with speech and language challenges to communicate effectively through speech. It can include physical exercises to improve the muscles used in speech as well as improving clarity.

SPINA BIFIDA A condition where the bones of the spine do not completely close around the spinal cord of a baby during pregnancy.

STEREOTYPE A generalised assumption about a person or a group of people based on limited knowledge or understanding.

TRANSGENDER Someone whose gender identity differs from the gender they were assigned at birth.

VENTILATOR A machine that helps someone to breathe, or that breathes for them.

INDEX

A Beautiful Mind 16
Academy Award (Oscar) 23
achondroplasia 29
activist 12, 25, 34, 48
actor 25, 29
Adepitan, Ade 47
advocate 12, 30
Ait Chitt, Redouan (Redo) 40–41
Akers, Michelle 58
alphabet grid 53
America (USA) 11, 16, 23, 29, 32, 34, 38, 39, 46, 50, 57
American Civil Liberties Union 12
Antigua 57
anxiety 20, 39, 50
appendicitis 8
artist 8, 15, 23, 50, 58
astronomer 32
athlete 26, 42, 46–47, 58
author 11, 12, 39, 45, 47, 53
autism 20, 53

Bedwei, Farida 44–45
Beethoven, Ludwig van 4–5
blind 12, 23, 32, 46
break-dancer 41
brittle bone disease 48
bulimia 39

Canada 26
cancer 8, 26
Caribbean 45, 57
Carter, Dwayne Jr. 58
cerebral palsy 45, 57
chemotherapy 26
comedian 48
comic book 34, 45
composer 5
Convention on the Rights of Persons with Disabilities 30
Costa Rica 30
Crohn's disease 59
crutches 6, 42, 45

deaf 5, 12
depression 38, 39
designer 54
Devandas, Catalina 30–31
diabetic retinopathy 32
Díaz-Merced, Wanda 32–33
Dinklage, Peter 28–29
Doctor Who 25
Down Syndrome 54
DOWN TO XJABELLE 54
Dynamo 59

educator 12
Emmy Award 29
England 5, 39, 25; see also UK
epilepsy 58
equal rights 15
Everest 37
explorer 37

fibromyalgia 50
"Fingertips" 23
footballer 58
Fox, Terry 26–27
France 8
Frayne, Steven 59

Game of Thrones 29
Germanotta, Stefani 50–51
Germany 5
Ghana 42, 45
Golden Globe Award 29
Graeae 25
Grammy Award 23
Grandin, Temple 20–21
Guatemala 54

Haig, Matt 39
hand sign 12
Hawking, Stephen 18–19
hidden disabilities 58–59
Higashida, Naoki 52–53
Holland 41
hospital 15, 16, 20, 23, 25, 37

India 37
"It's Our Story" 34

Jacobsson, Jonas 46
Japan 53
Jordan 25

Kahlo, Frida 14–15
Karmzah 45
Keller, Helen 12–13
Kirchhoff, Gustav 6–7

Lady Gaga 50–51
lawyer 30, 38
leg calliper 47
Lil Wayne 58
Lincoln, Abraham 38
London Fashion Week 54
Lovato, Demi 39

magician 59
marathon 26
mathematician 16, 19
Matisse, Henri 8–9
ME (Chronic Fatigue Syndrome) 58
medal 46, 58
mental health 16, 38–39
Mexico 15
model 8, 54, 57
motor-neurone disease 19
mountaineer 37

Nash, John 16–17
National Theatre 25
Nobel Memorial Prize 16

Olympics 42, 58
osteogenesis imperfecta 25, 48
osteomalacia 11

painting 8, 15
Paralympics 46–47
Perkins School for the Blind 12
Philip, Aaron 56–57
physicist 6, 19, 32
Pineda, Victor 34–35
polio 15, 34, 47
President of the USA 38
professor 20
prosthetic leg 26, 37, 42
Puerto Rico 32

rapper 58
Reasons to Stay Alive 39
Russia 6

scholar 16, 34
Shaban, Nabil 24–25
Shadows and Sunshine 11
Silver Scorpion 34
singer-songwriter 23, 39, 50, 58
Sinha, Arunima 36–37
software engineer 45
speech therapy 20
spina bifida 30
sport shooter 46
Springmuhl Tejada, Isabella 54–55
Suggs, Eliza 10–11
Sullivan, Anne 12
Svenska Dagbladet Gold Medal 46
Sweden 46
swimmer 46

teacher 11, 12, 19, 20,25, 26, 34, 41, 48
TED Talk 32, 48
The Reason I Jump 53
The Story of My Life 12
transgender 57
TV presenter 47

UK 45, 46; see also England
university 6, 16, 19, 20, 25, 26, 34, 46

Venezuela 34
ventilator 34

wheelchair 6, 8, 11, 25, 26, 30, 34, 46, 47, 48, 57
wheelchair basketball 26, 47
women's rights 12, 30
Wonder, Stevie 22–23
World Enabled 34
writer 25

Young, Stella 48–49
Yeboah, Emmanuel Ofosu 42–43

Zorn, Trischa 46

USEFUL SOURCES

If you want to read more about the things covered in this book or if you need some more support or guidance then below is a collection of sources including books, websites and blogs that you might find interesting

WEBSITES

YA reviewed by a young disabled person:
http://thebookaddictedgirl.blogspot.com/

Bookmark, the Booktrust site on disability and books:
https://www.booktrust.org.uk/books-and-reading/bookmark-disability-and-books/

Carefully curated books featuring disabled characters:
www.letterboxlibrary.com

Information about identity-first language and why it's used:
https://autisticadvocacy.org/about-asan/identity-first-language/

BOOKS

The Reason I Jump – Naoki Higashida (Random House, 2013)

The Spectrum Girl's Survival Guide: How to Grow Up Awesome and Autistic – Siena Castellon (Jessica Kingsley Publishers, 2020)

***Ade's Amazing Ade-ventures* series** – Ade Adepitan (Studio Press, 2018)

Echo Boy – Matt Haig (Random House Children's Books, 2001)

A Boy Called Christmas – Matt Haig (Knopf Books for Young Readers, 2016)

MORE FROM CERRIE BURNELL

Snowflakes (Scholastic, 2013)

The Harper Series (Sky Pony, 2017)

The Girl With the Shark's Teeth (Oxford University Press, 2019)

The Ice Bear Miracle (Oxford University Press, 2019)

To my family for their unwavering support ~ L.B.

First Published in 2020 by Wide Eyed Editions, an imprint of The Quarto Group.
100 Cummings Center, Suite 265D, Beverly, MA 01915, USA.
T +1 978-282-9590 F +1 978-283-2742 www.QuartoKnows.com

A catalogue record for this book is available from the British Library.

ISBN 978-0-7112-4745-1

The illustrations were created digitally
Set in Vibur and Quicksand

Published by Georgia Amson-Bradshaw
Designed by Myrto Dimitrakoulia
Edited by Lucy Brownridge
Production by Dawn Cameron

Manufactured in Guangdong, China EB082020
9 8 7 6 5 4 3 2